Magic and Witchcraft

Volume 1

By Kelly Horton

Copyright 2018 Kelly Horton

ALL RIGHTS RESERVED

With the exception of those used in review's, the uncoloured or blank images herein, may not be reproduced, in whole or part by any means existing, other than for review.

The pages contained within are for personal use only. You may not distribute to or share uncoloured blank pages with any other colourists, in colouring groups, colouring group parties, via Email or message etc. to any other person, group, people or entity, and you may not upload blank or uncoloured pages to the internet without prior written permission of the artist and author Kelly Horton / The colouring Collective publications.

For any further details, including information on other books or colouring pages contact:

Kellyartistthorton@yahoo.com

For more colouring pages:

www.etsy.com/uk/Colourcollectiveshop

Join the Facebook Community: Search for the

The Colouring Collective

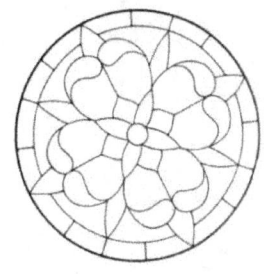
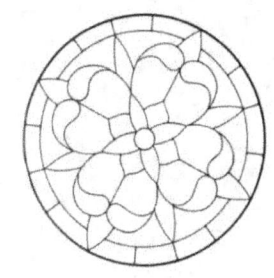

This book belongs to

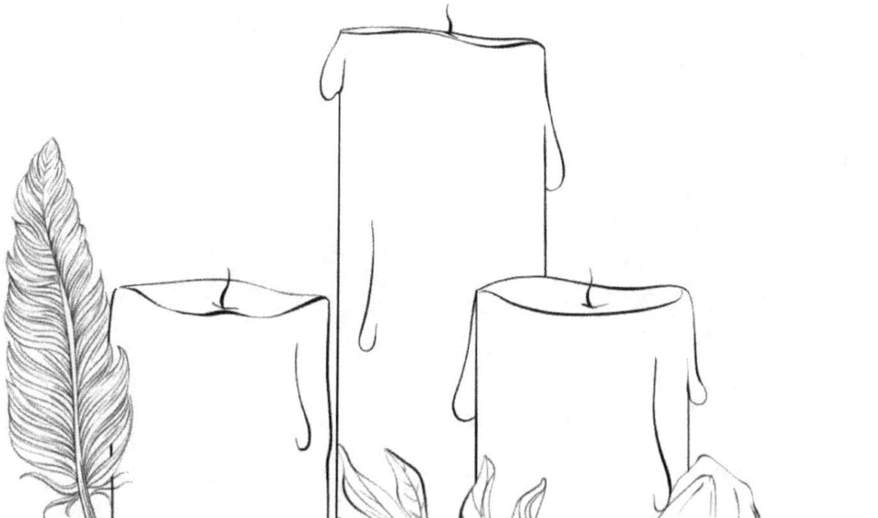

_____

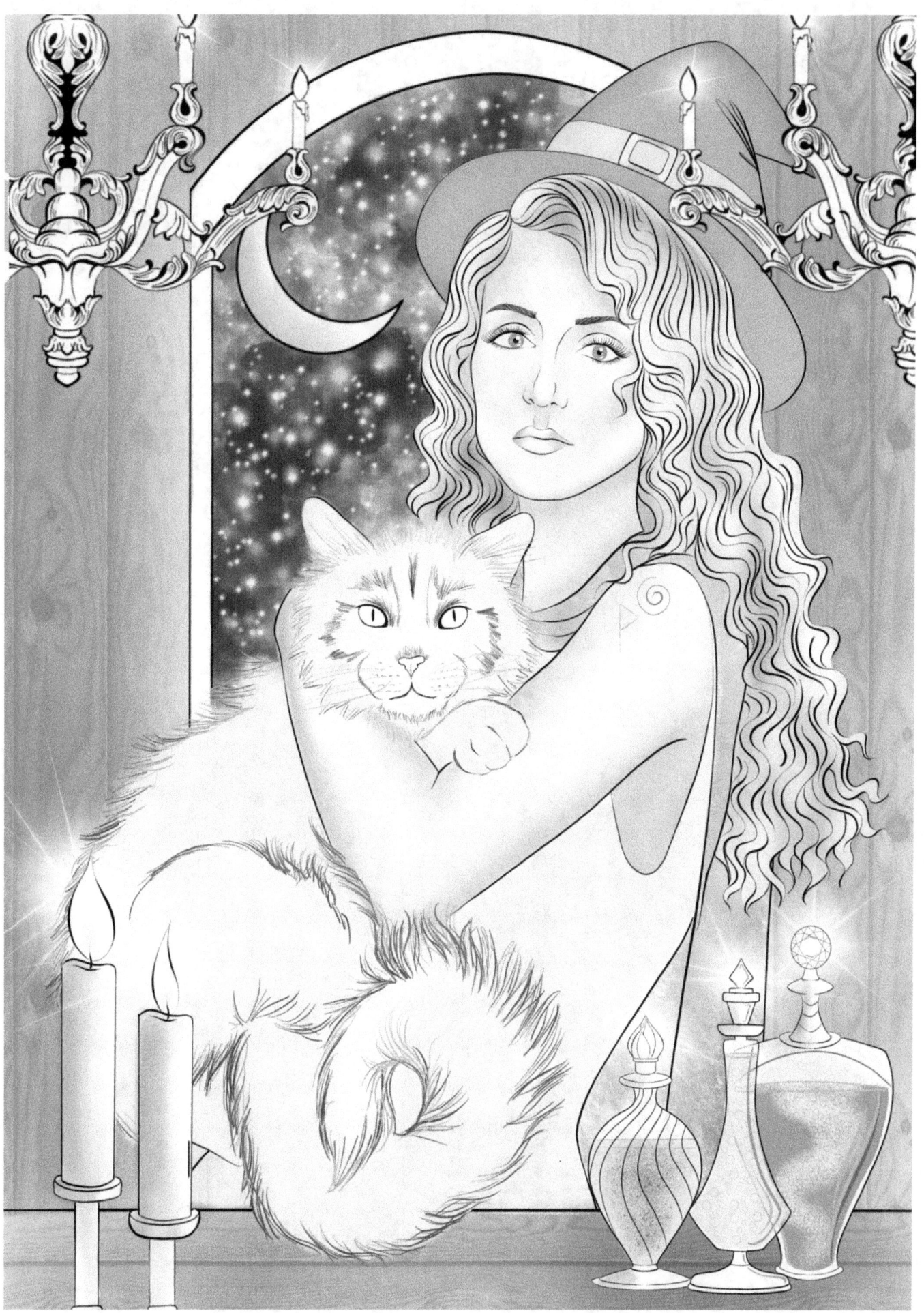

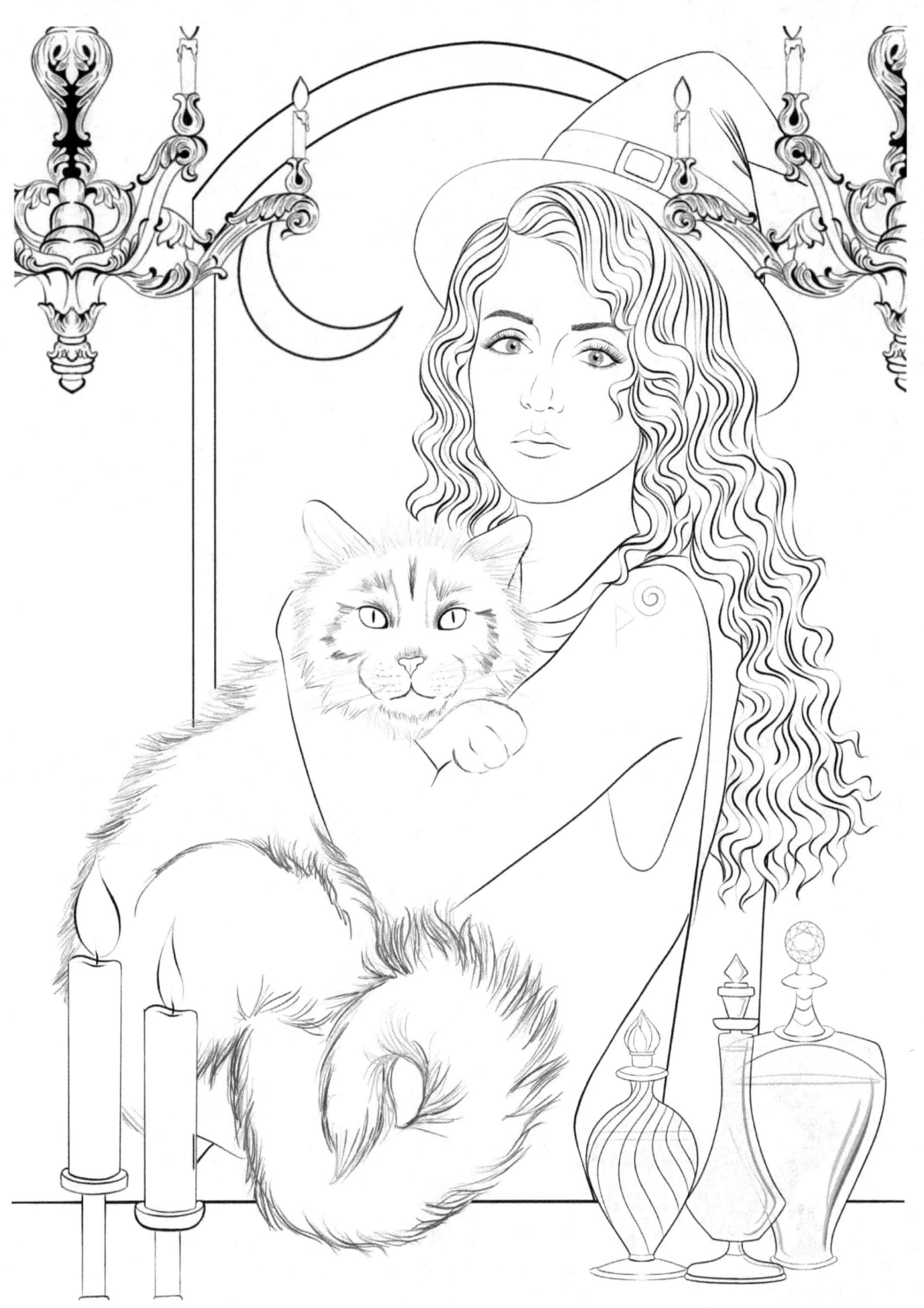

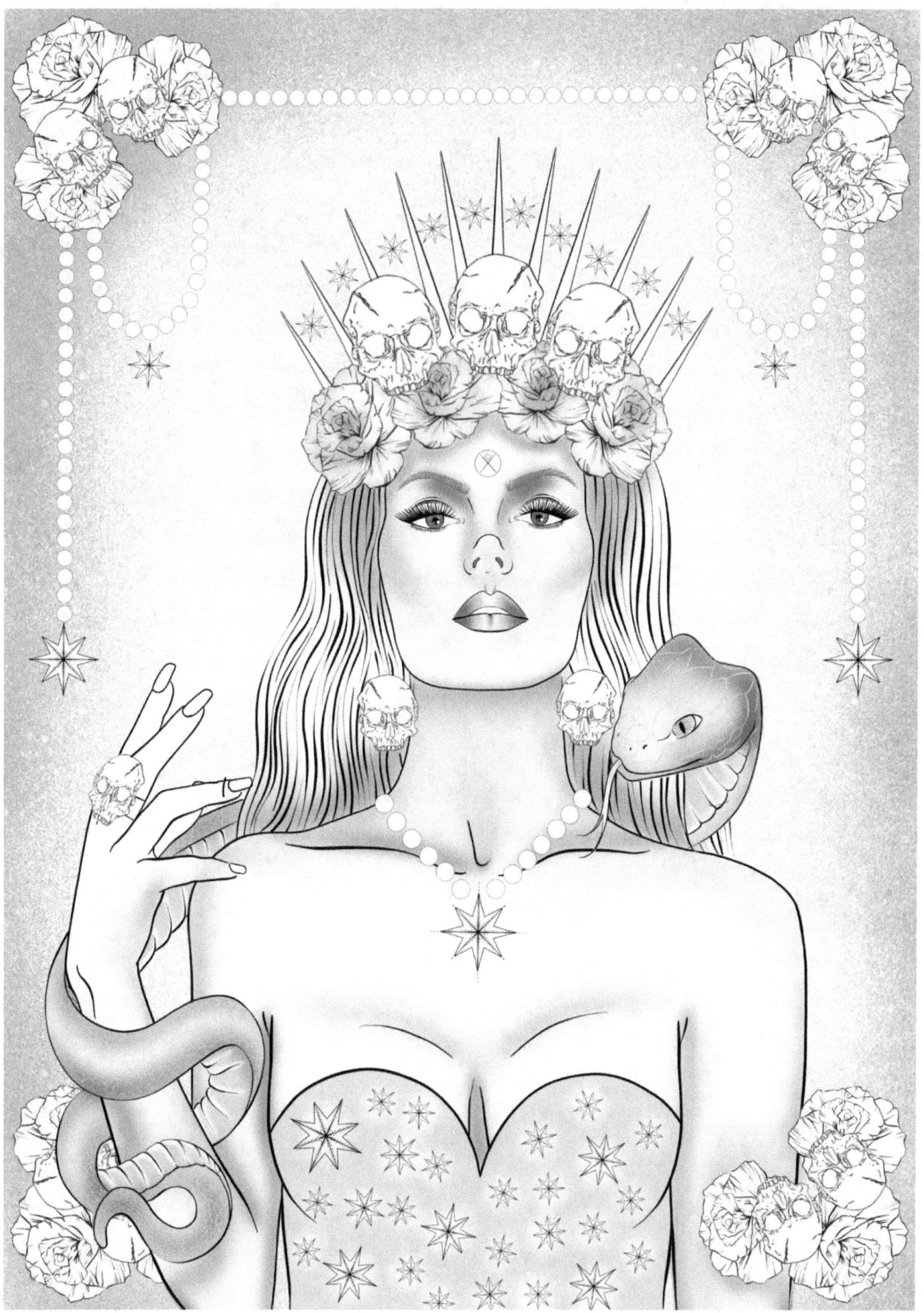

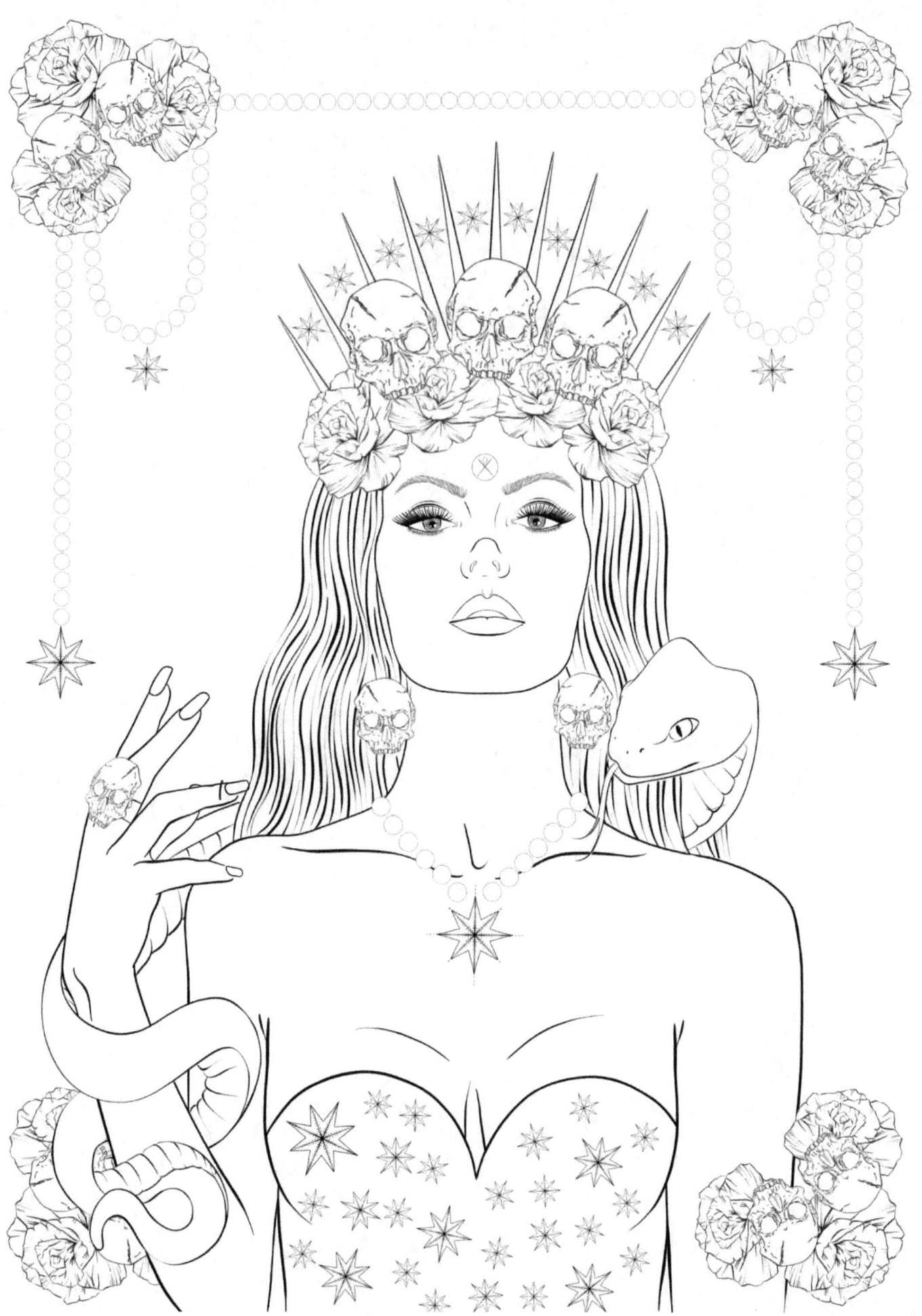

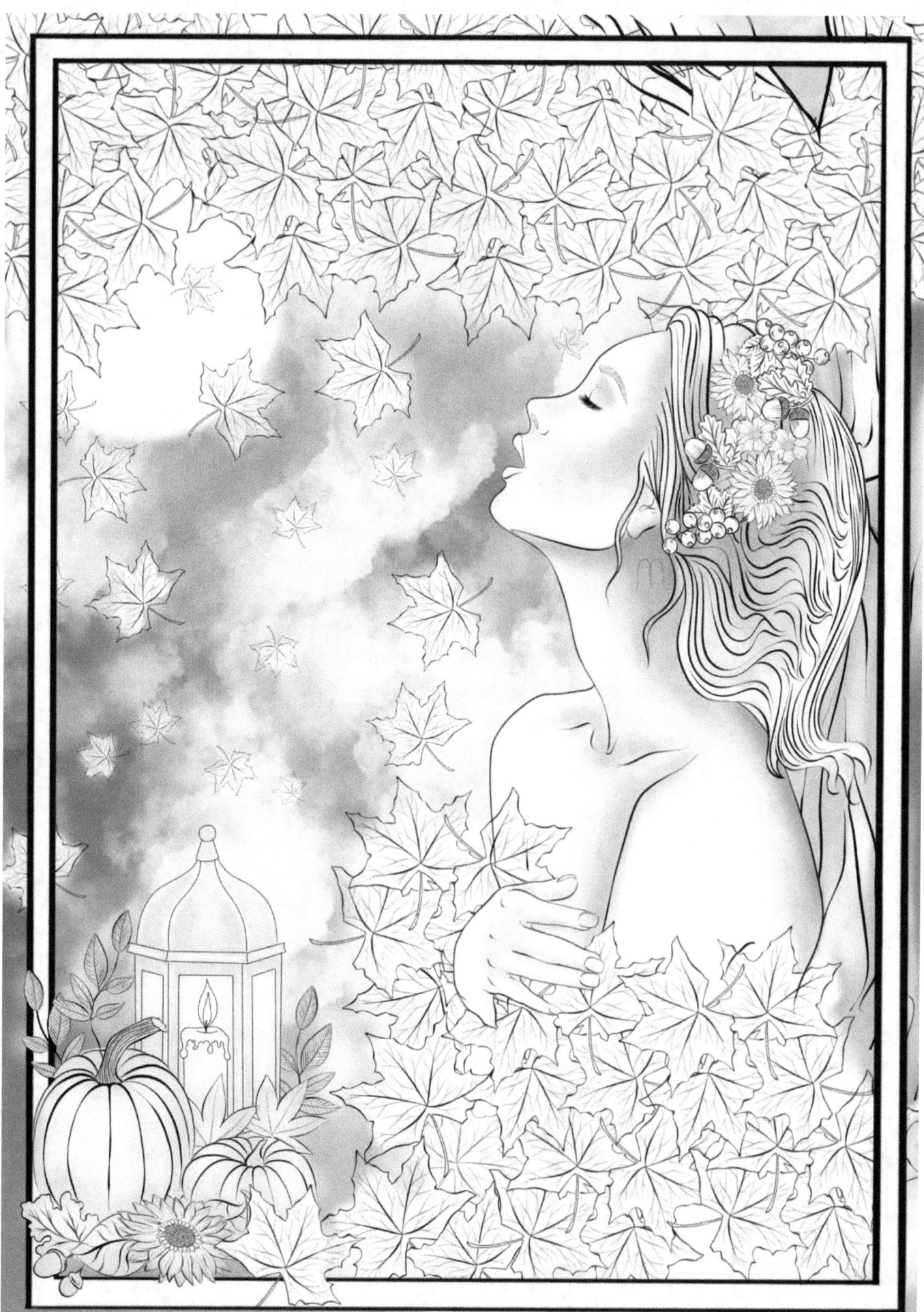

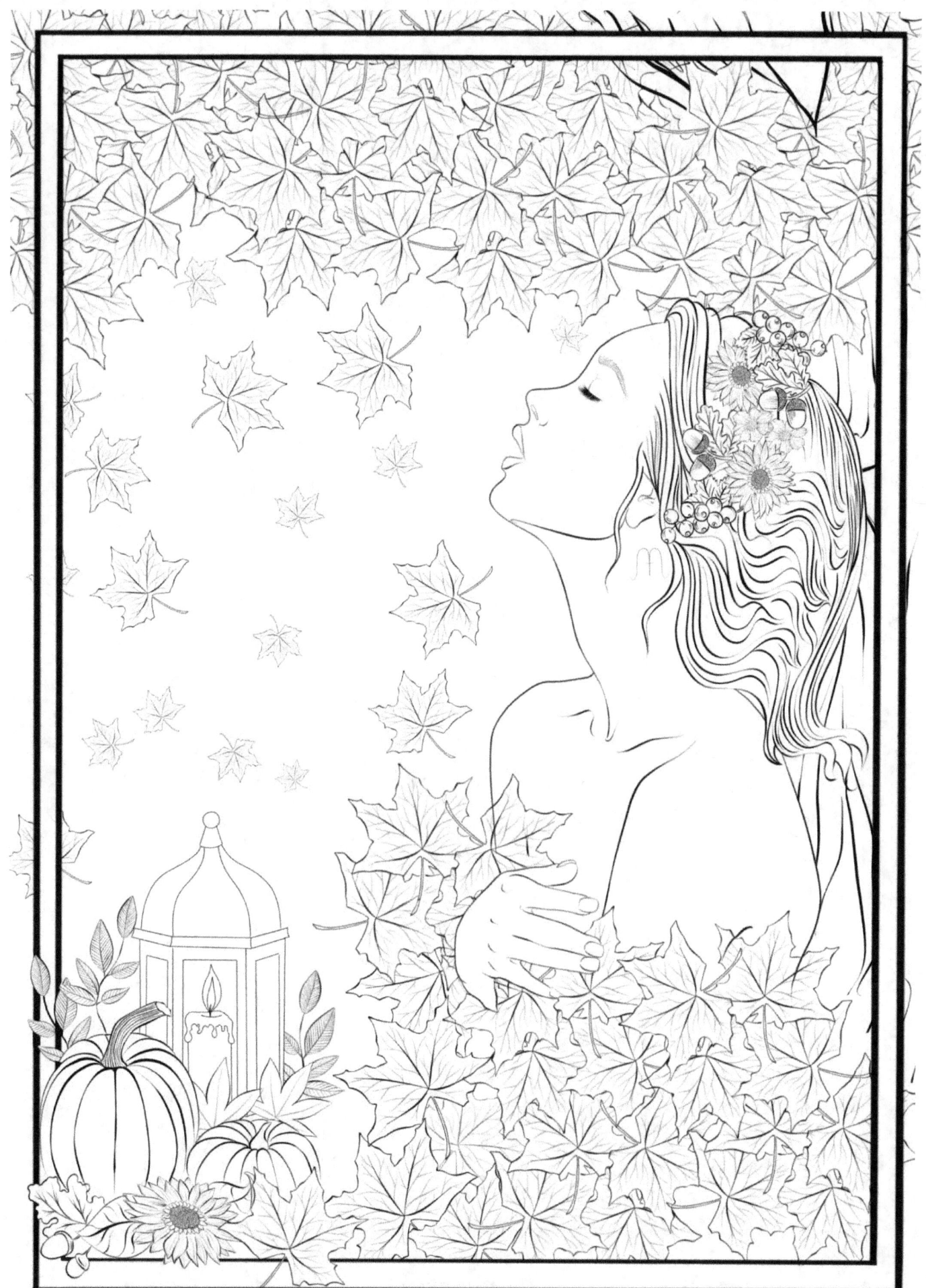

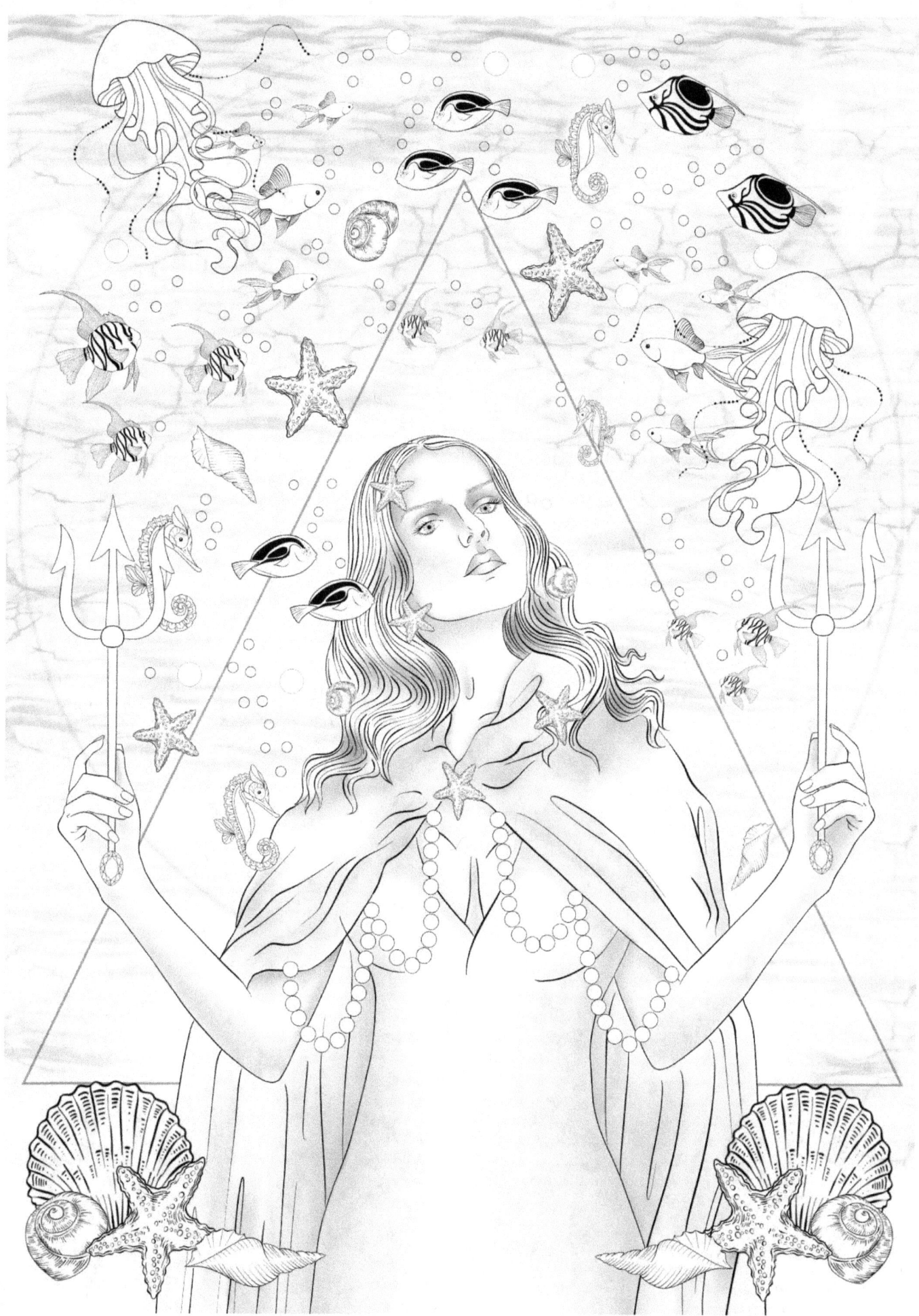

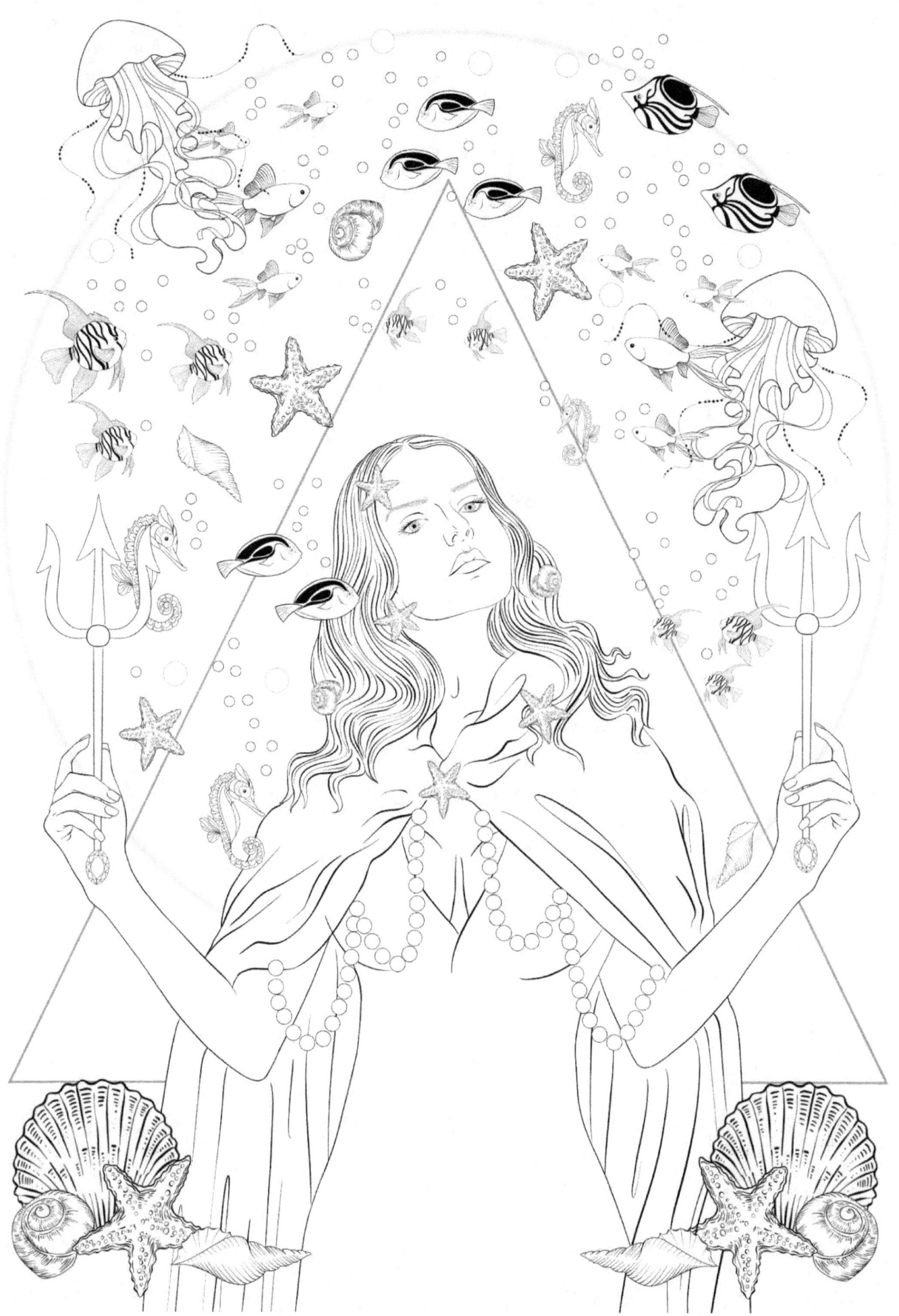

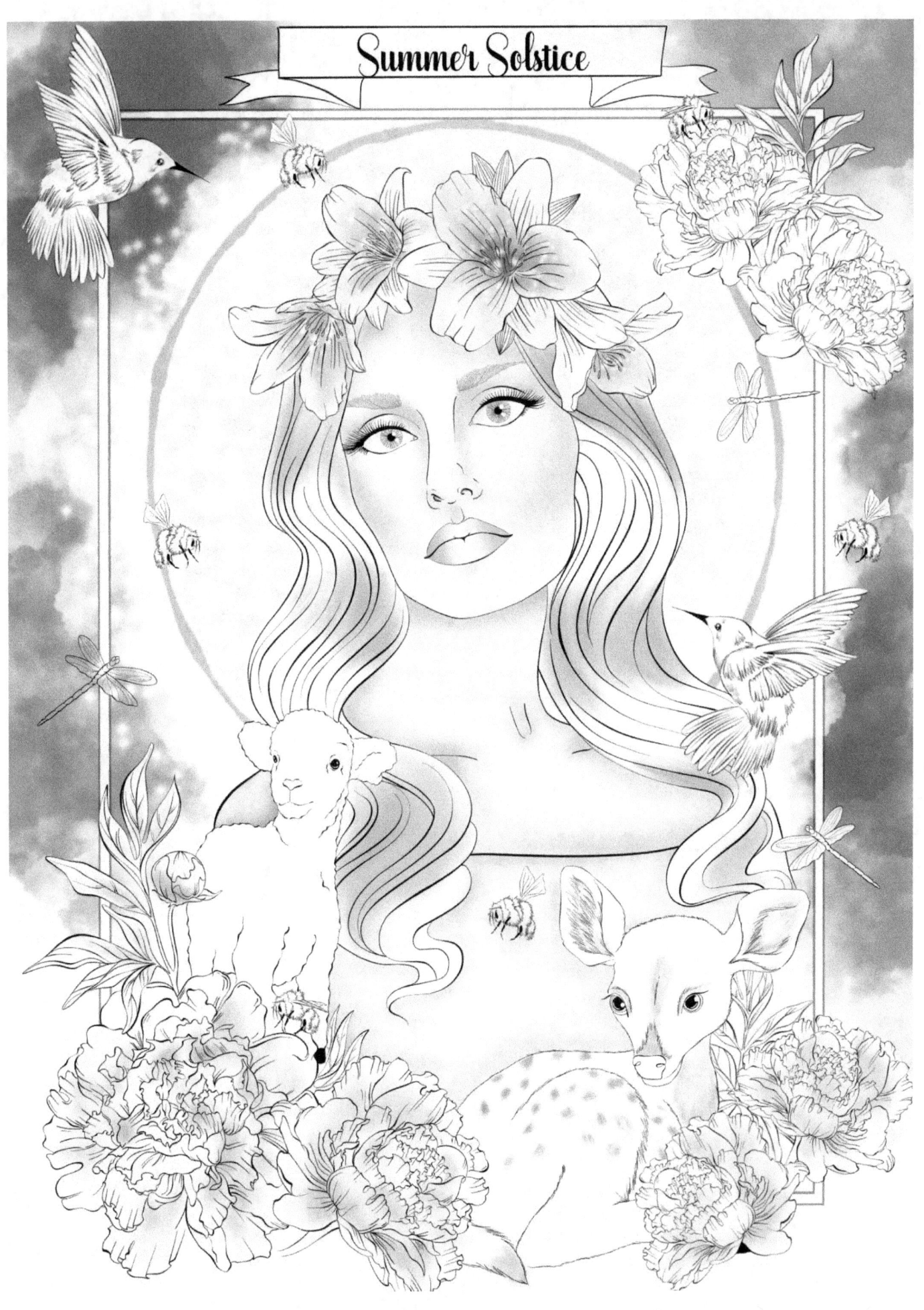

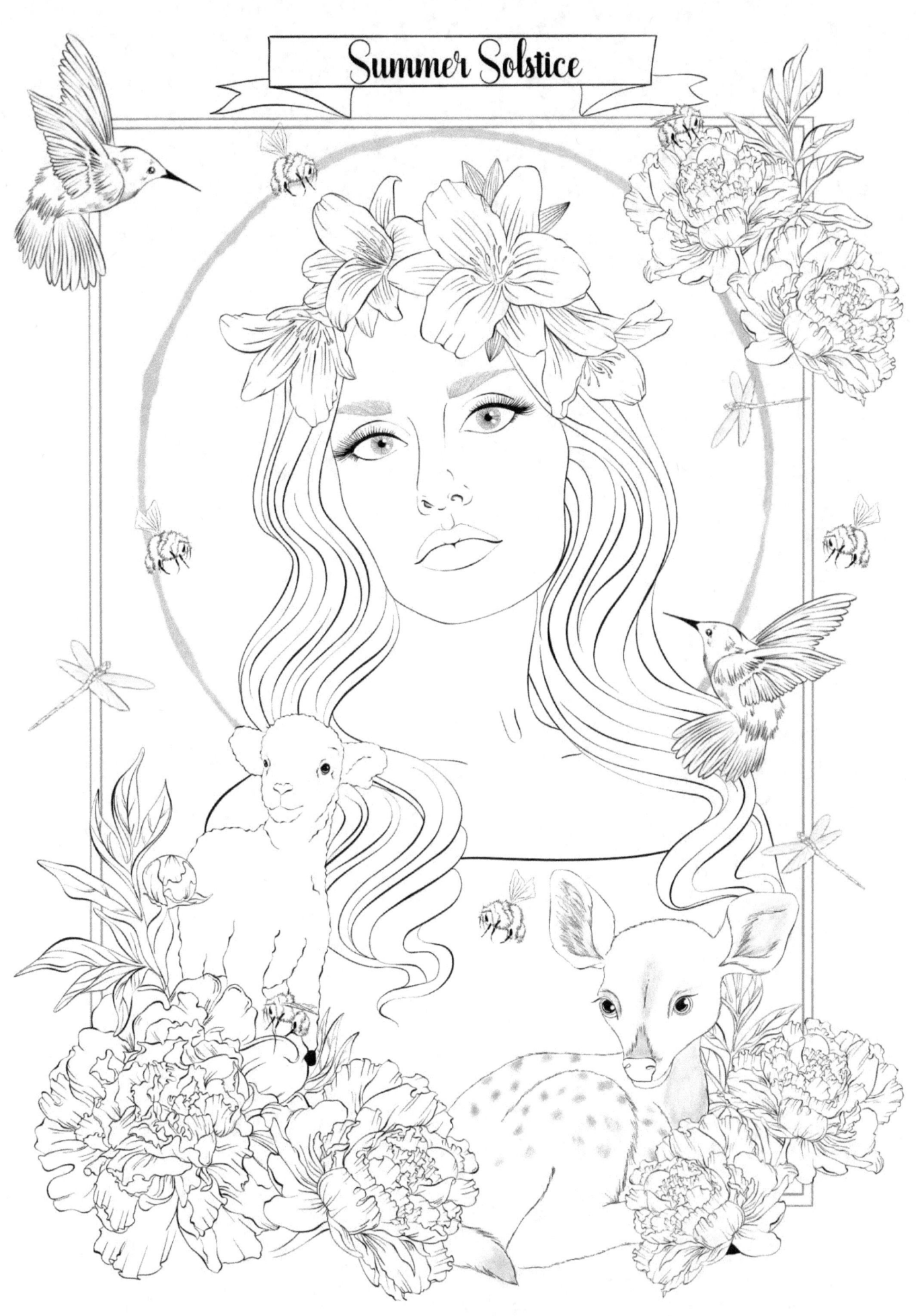

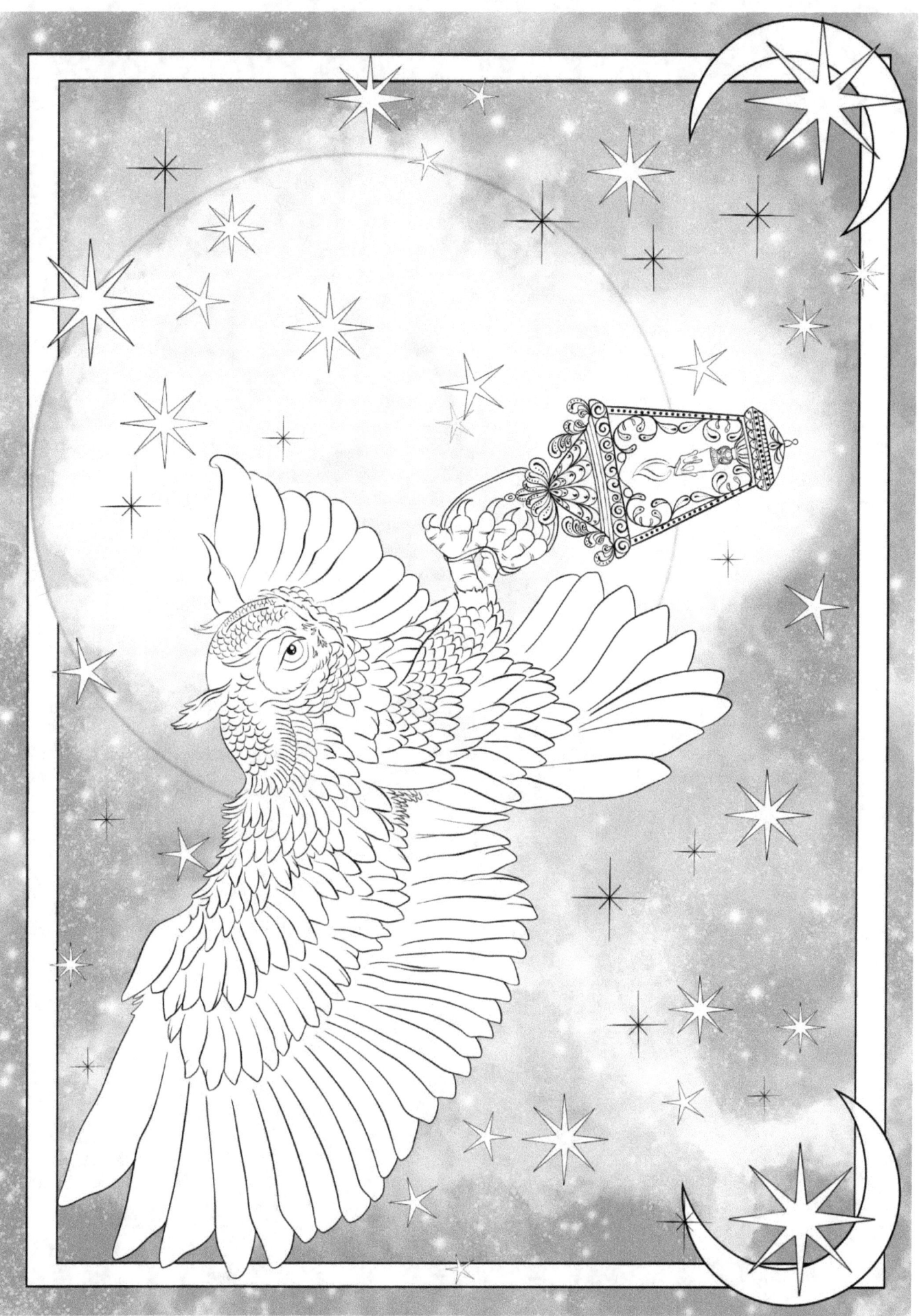

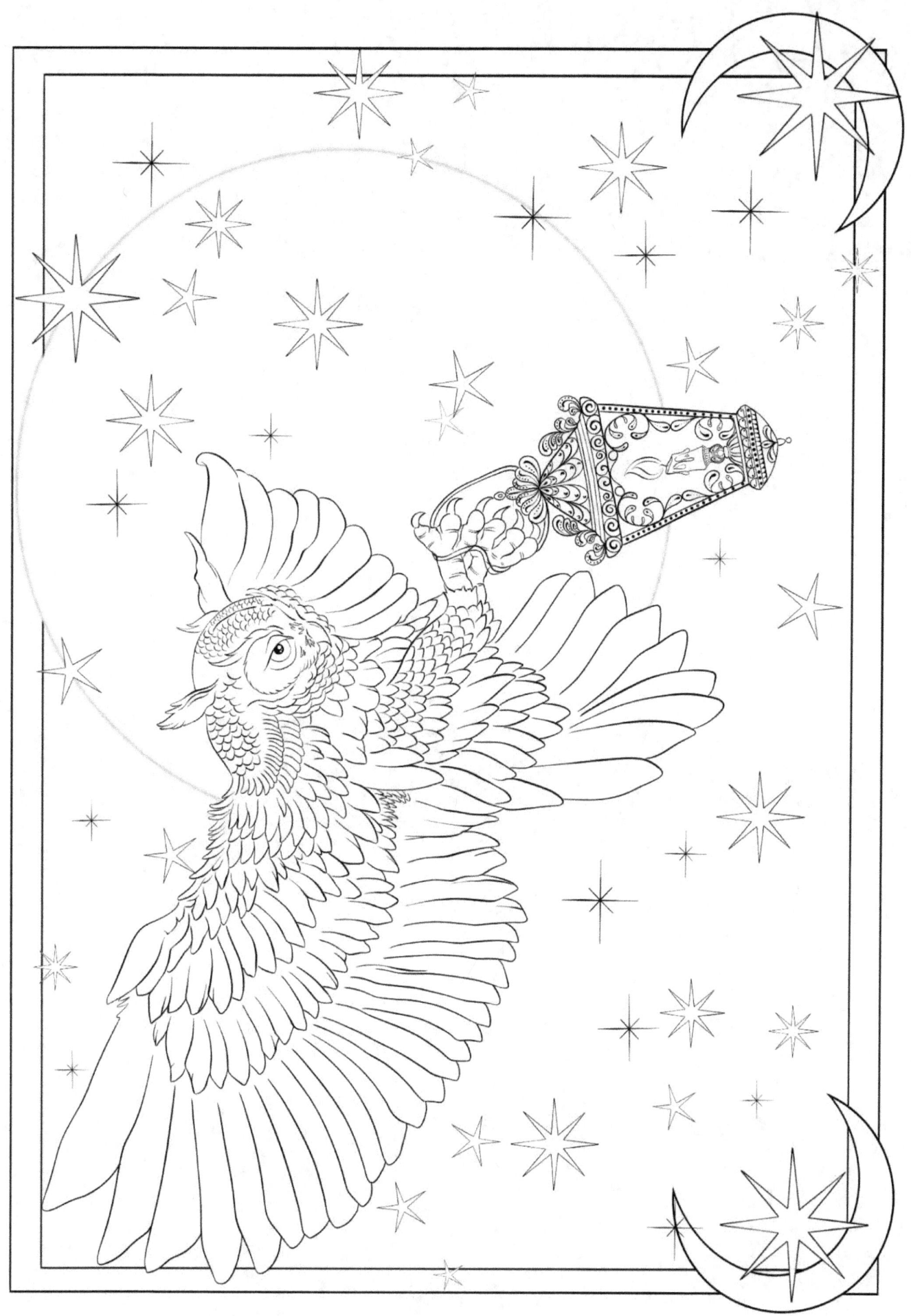

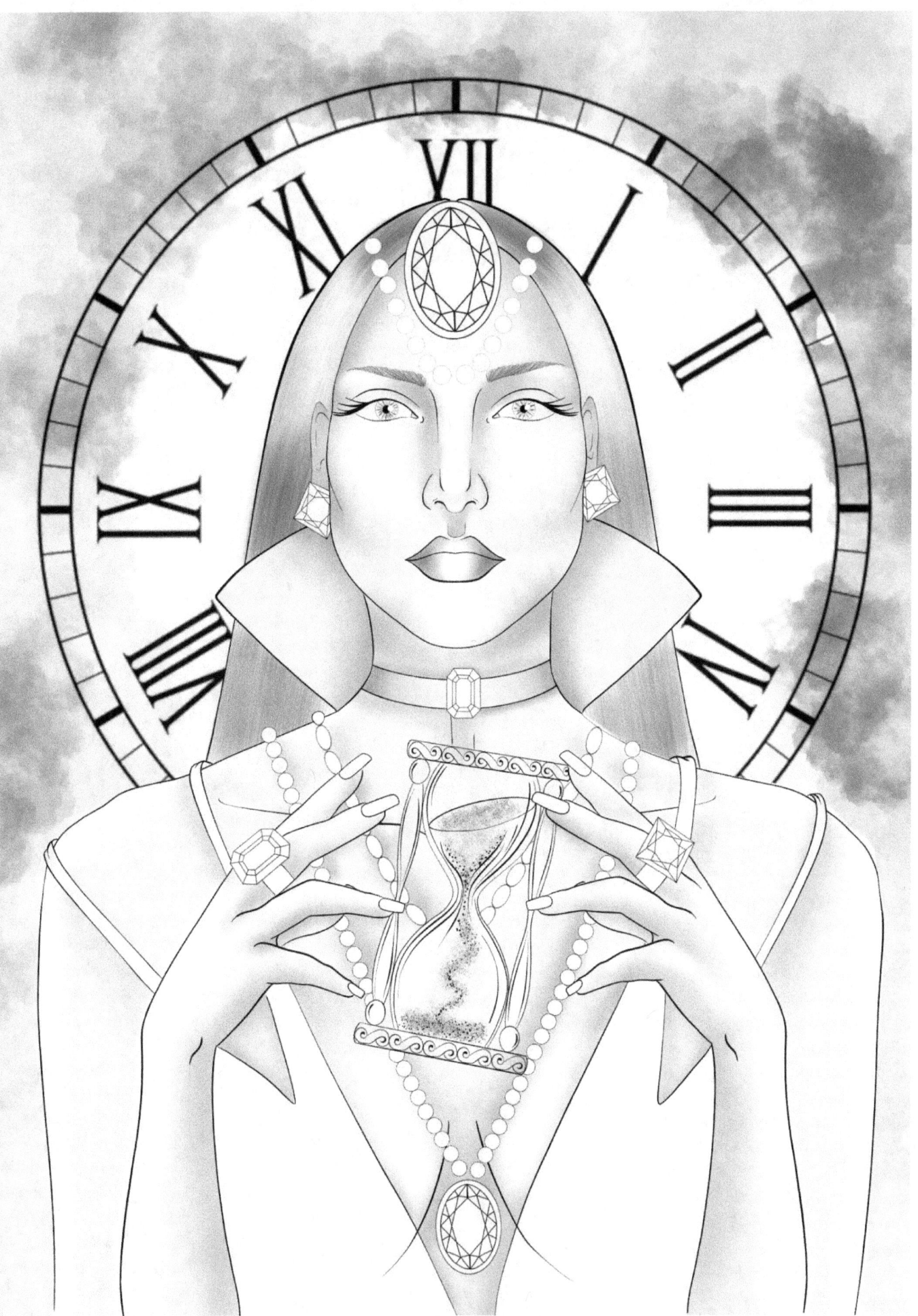

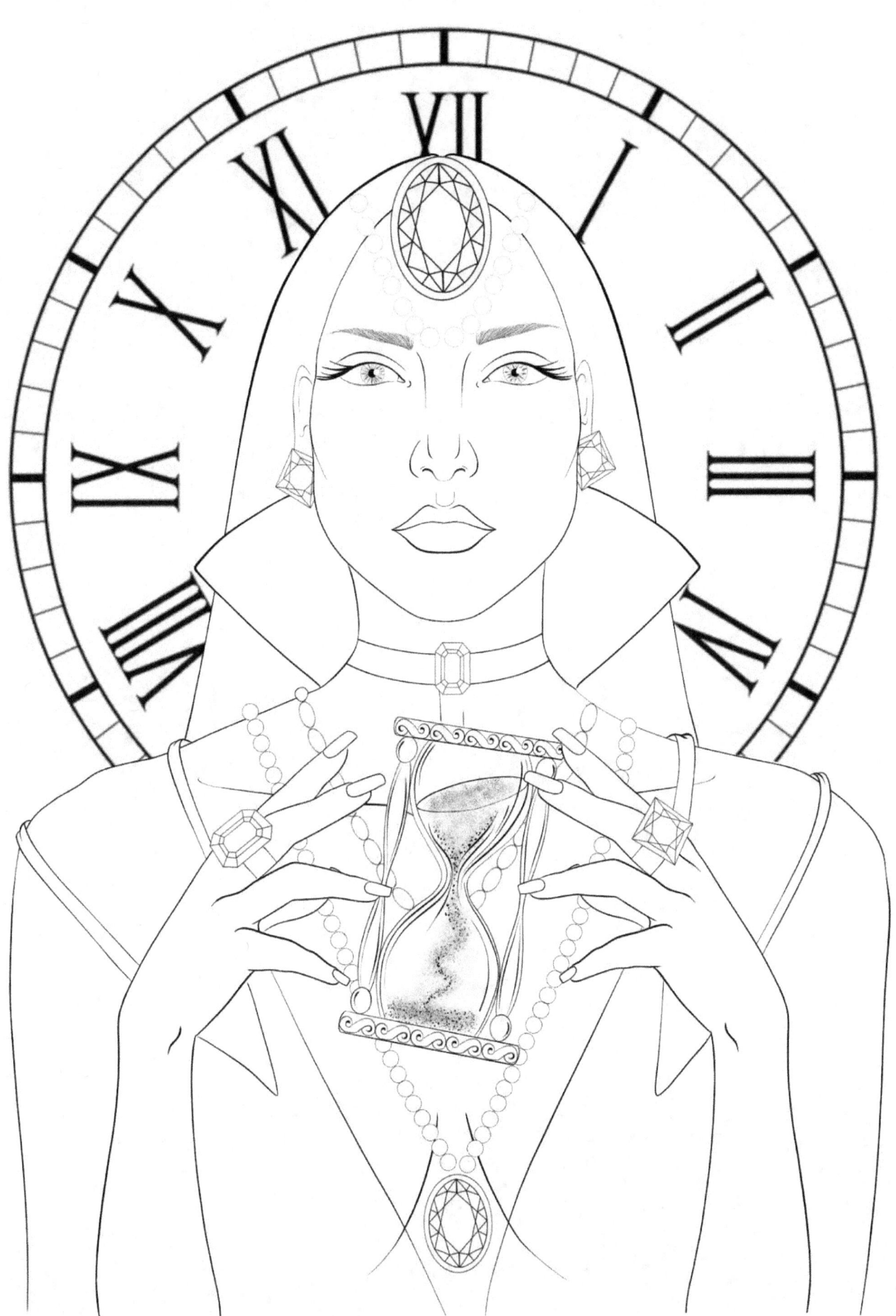

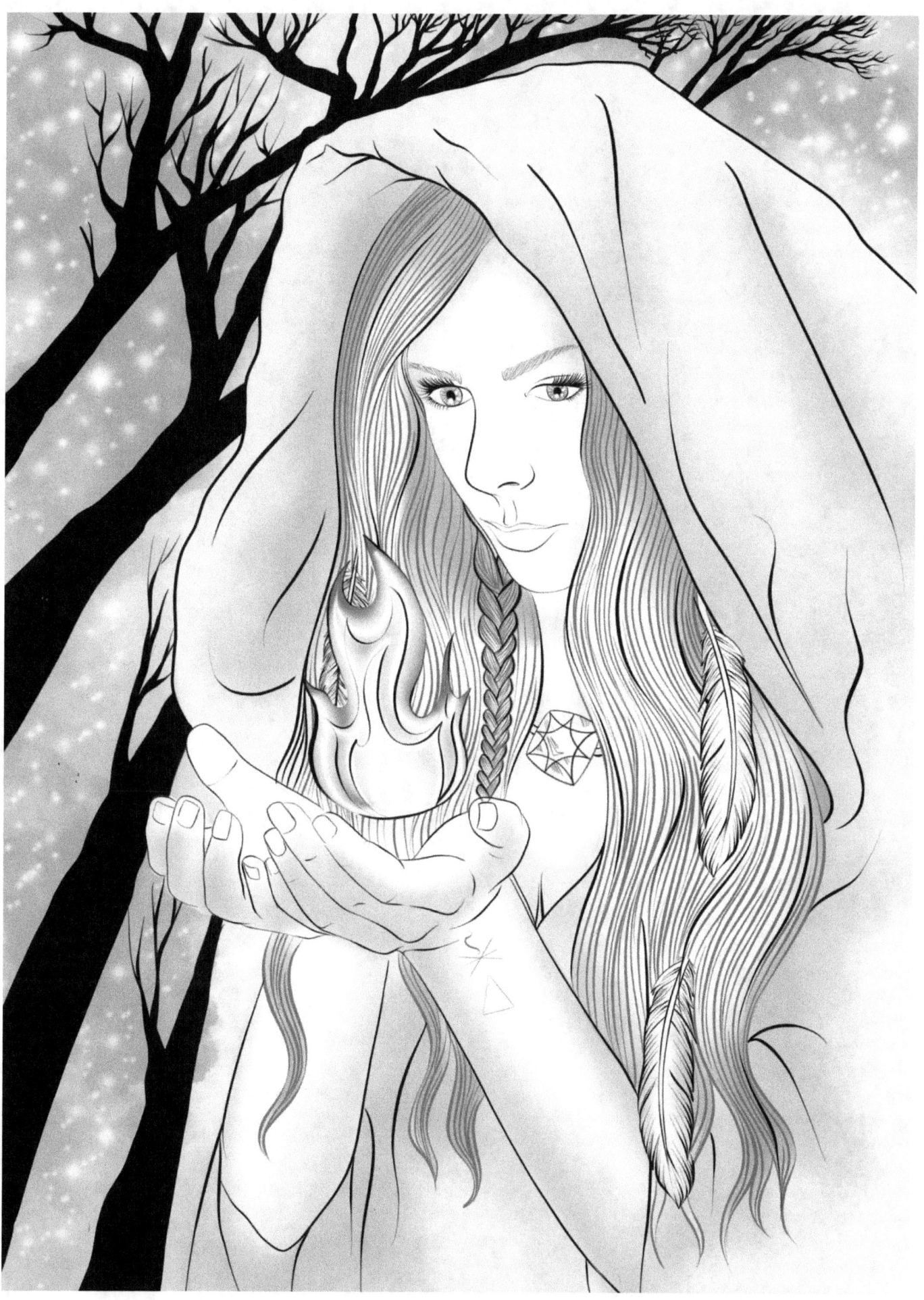

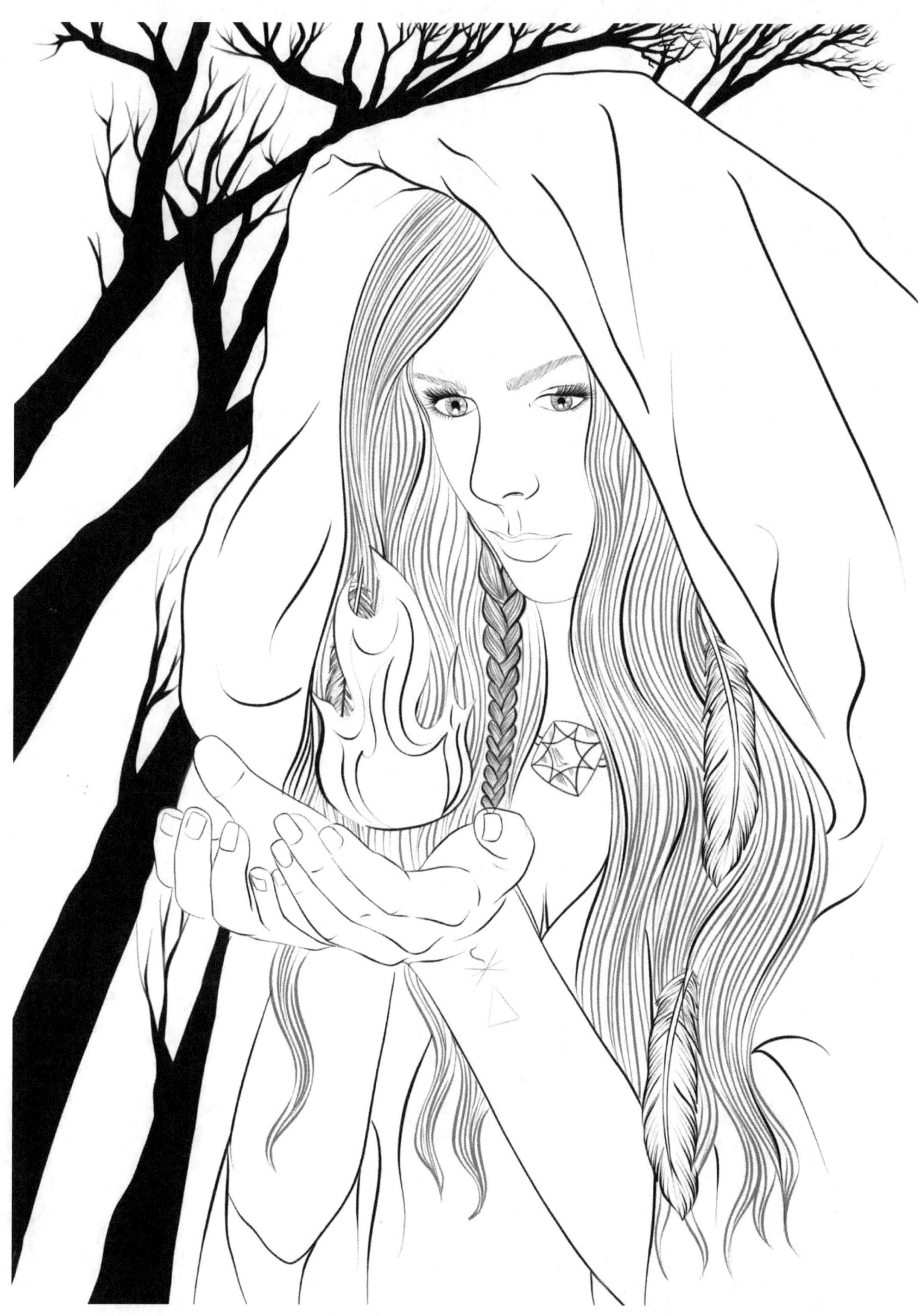

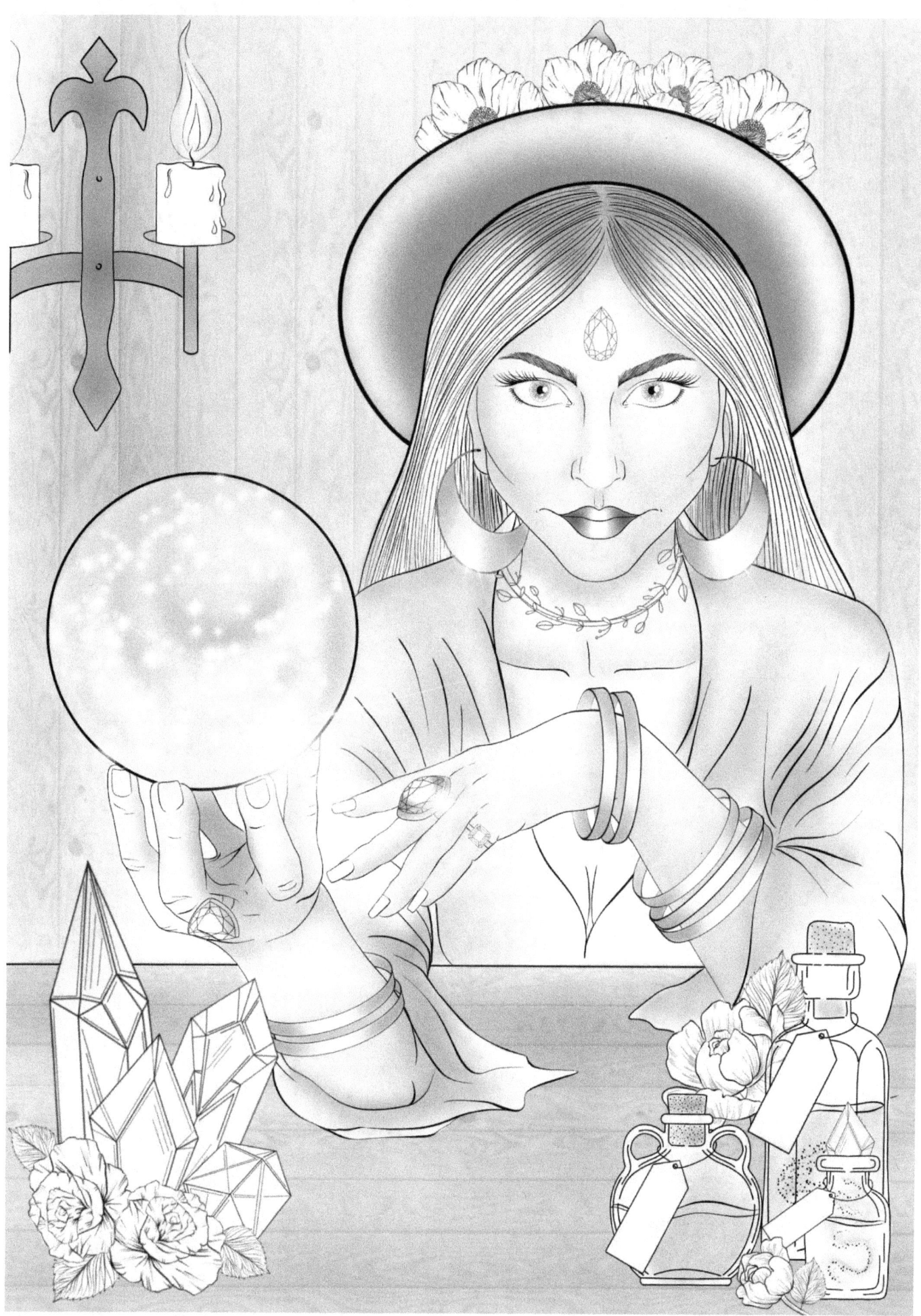

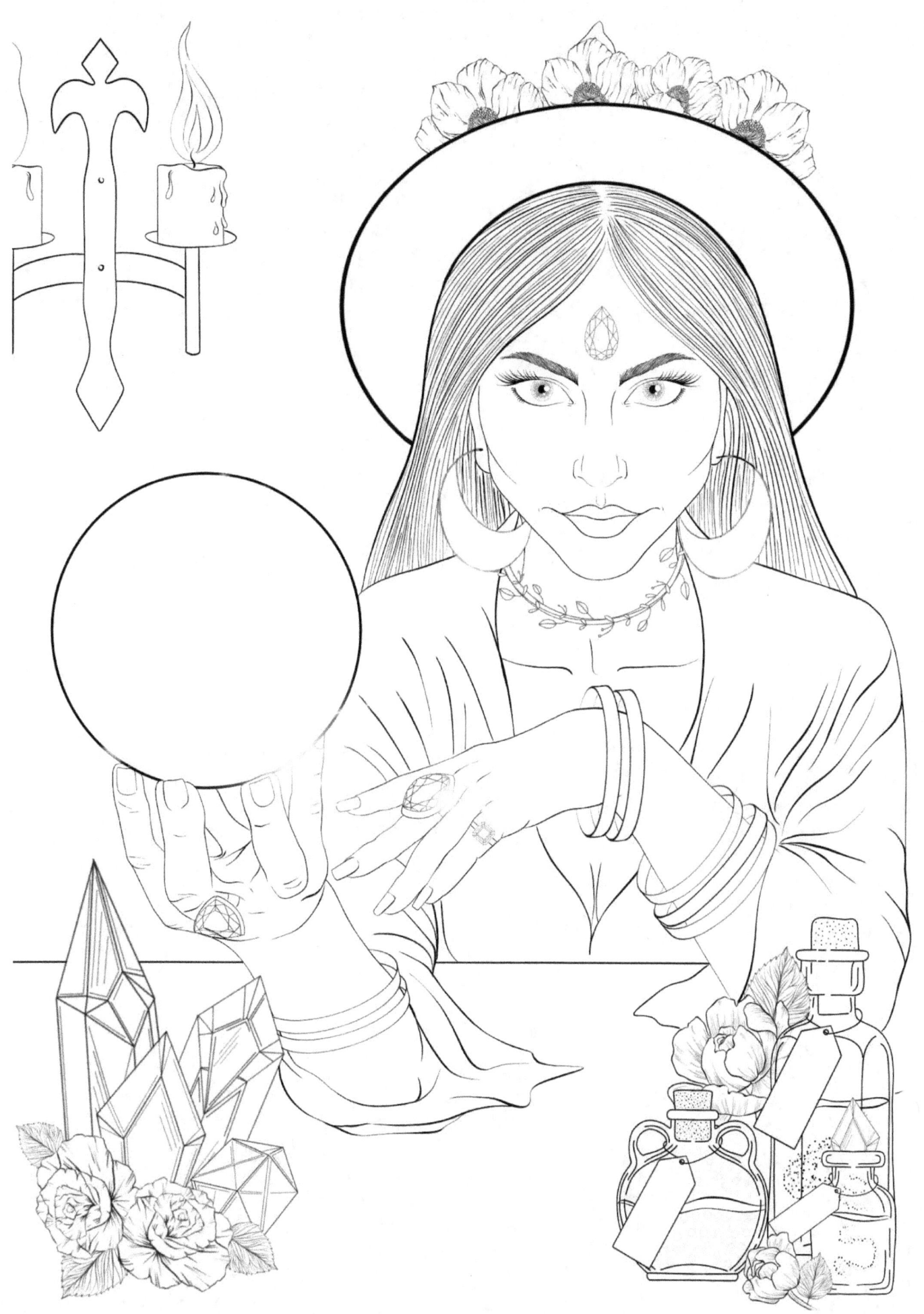

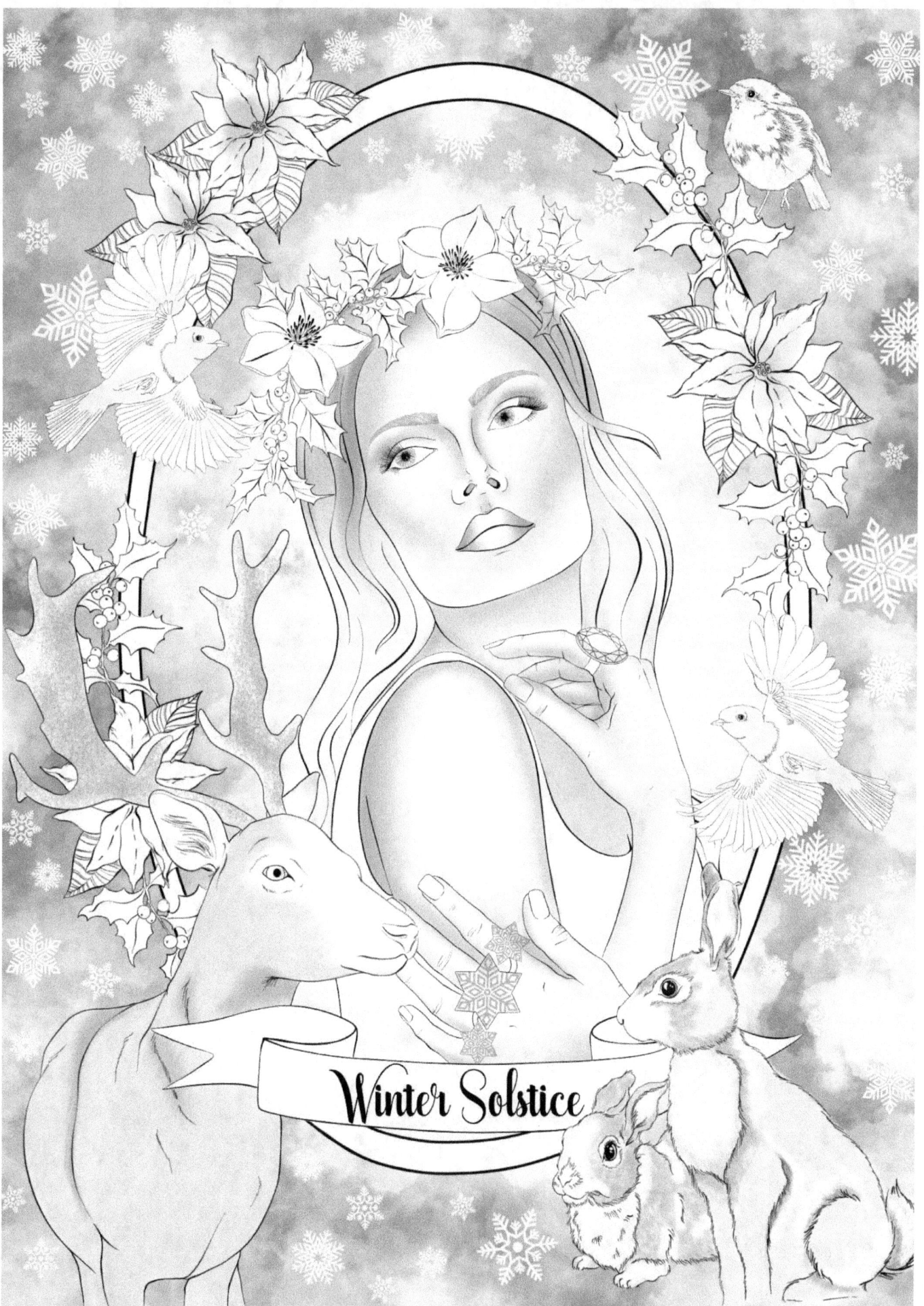

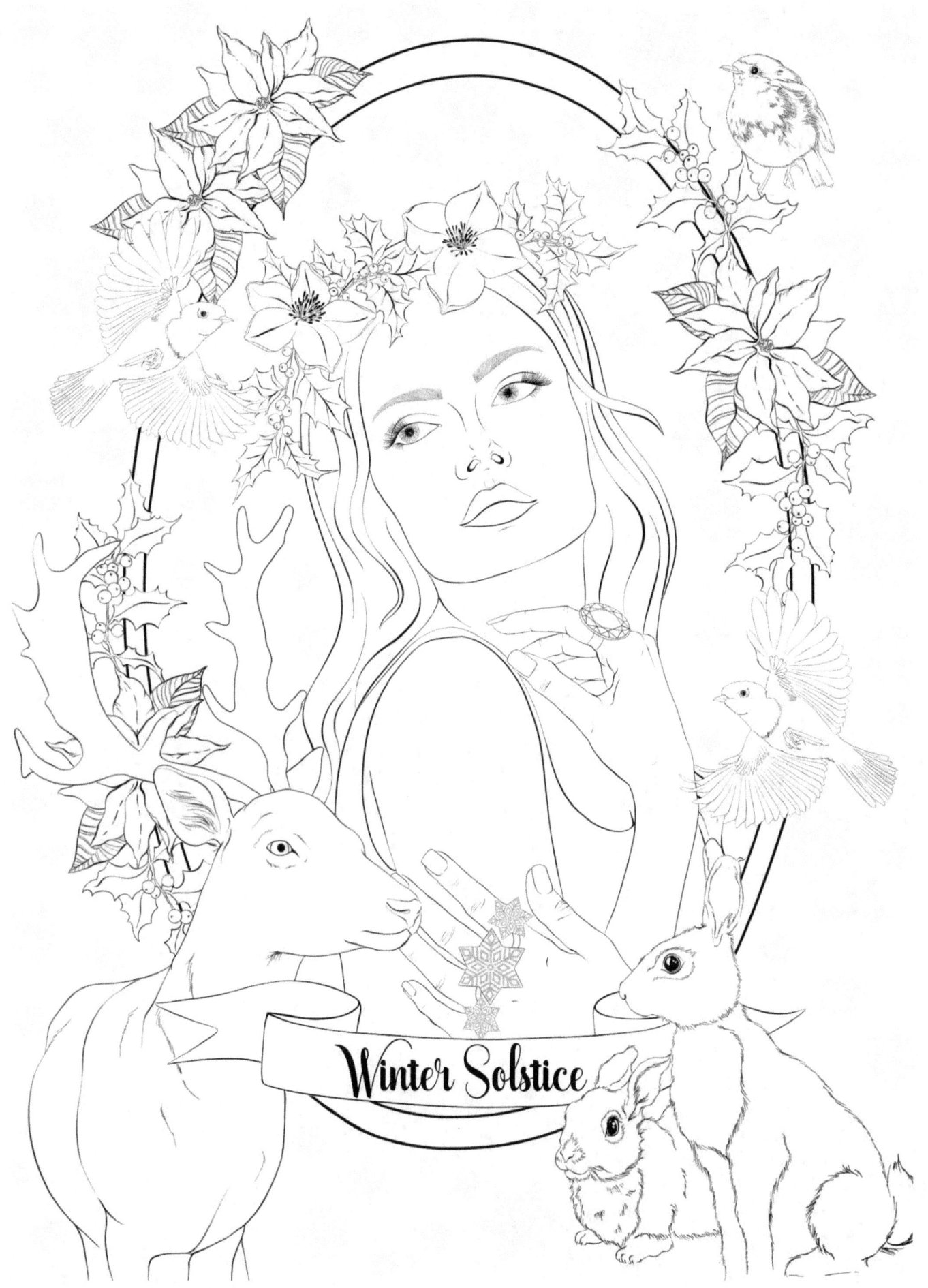

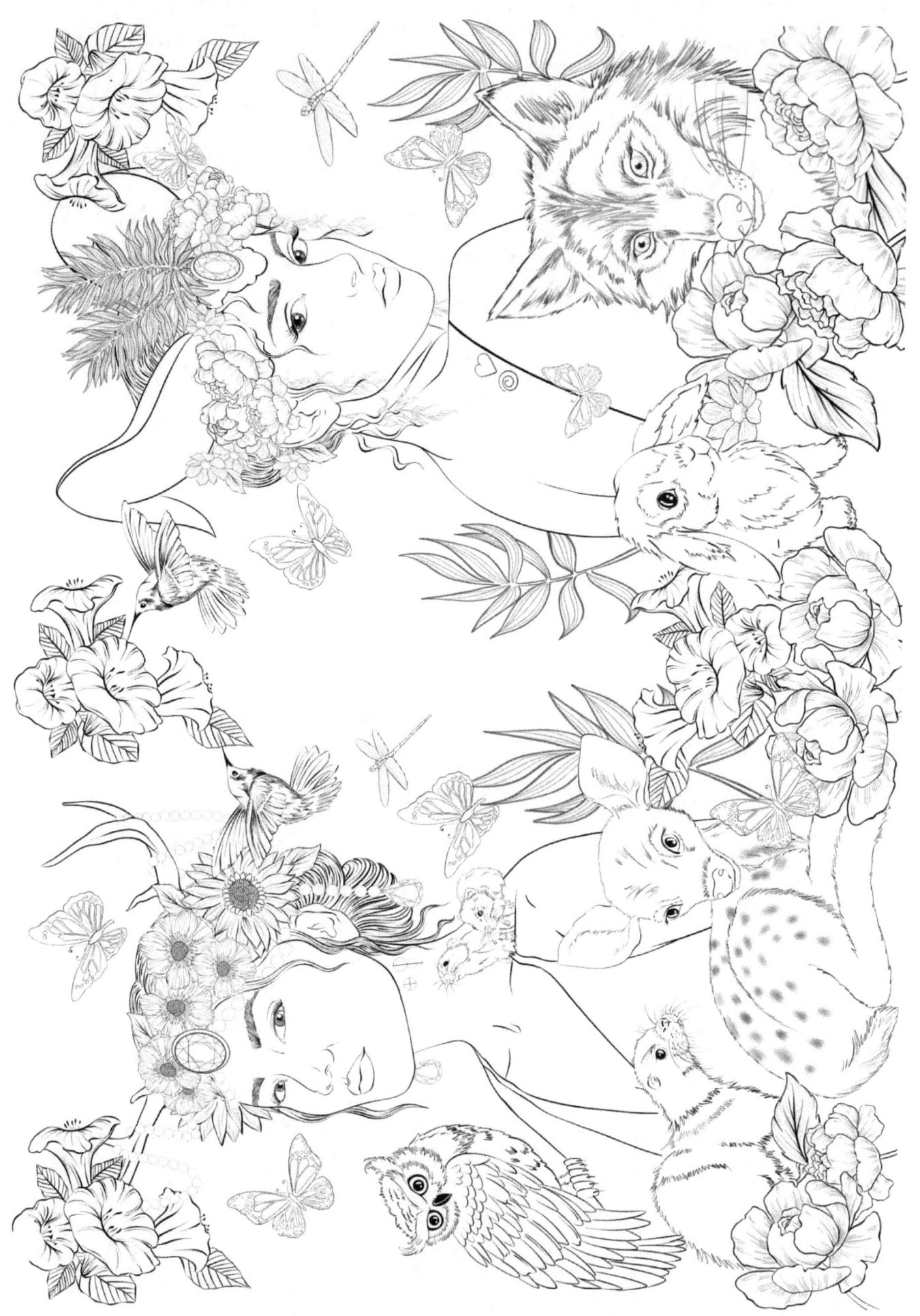

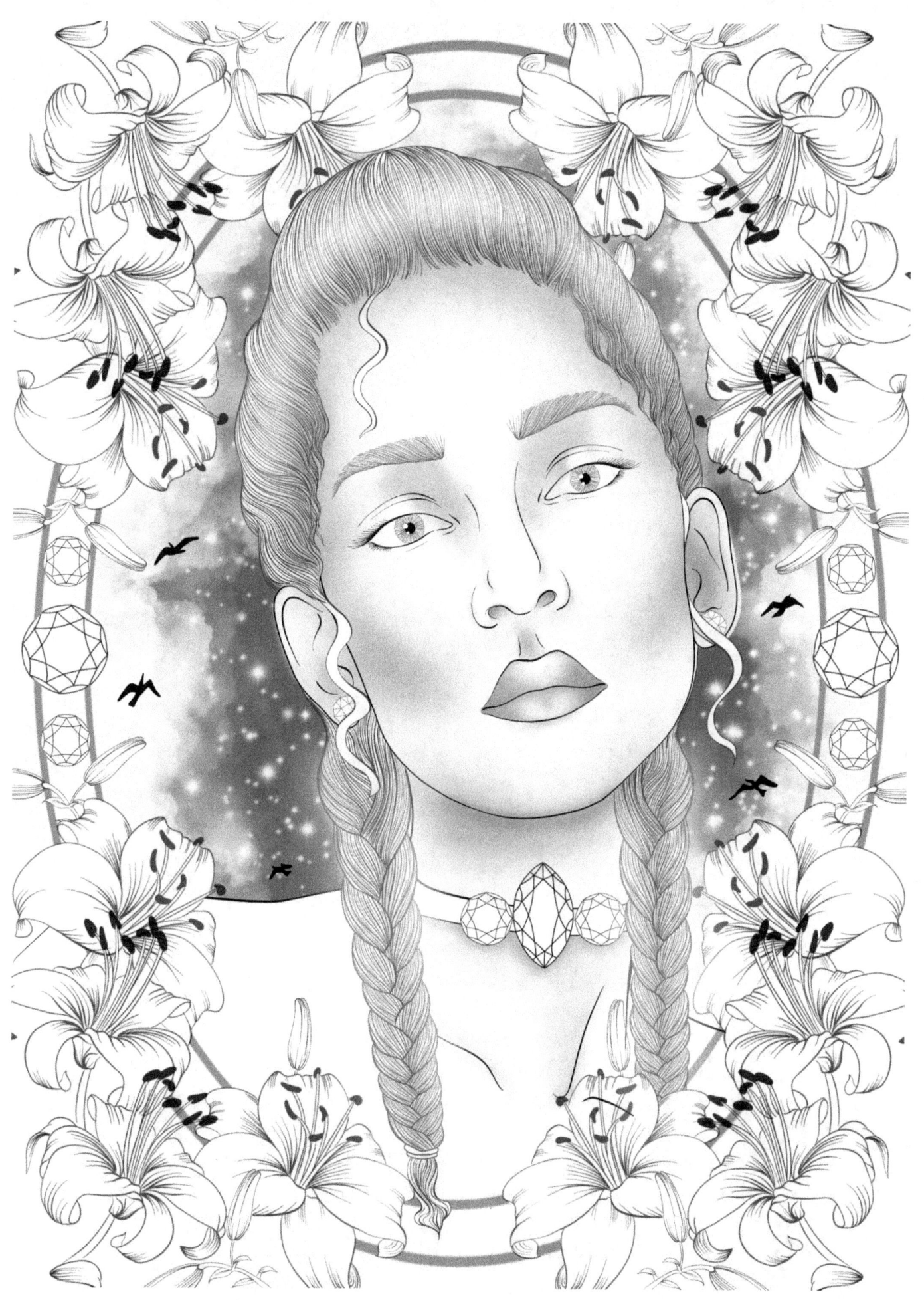

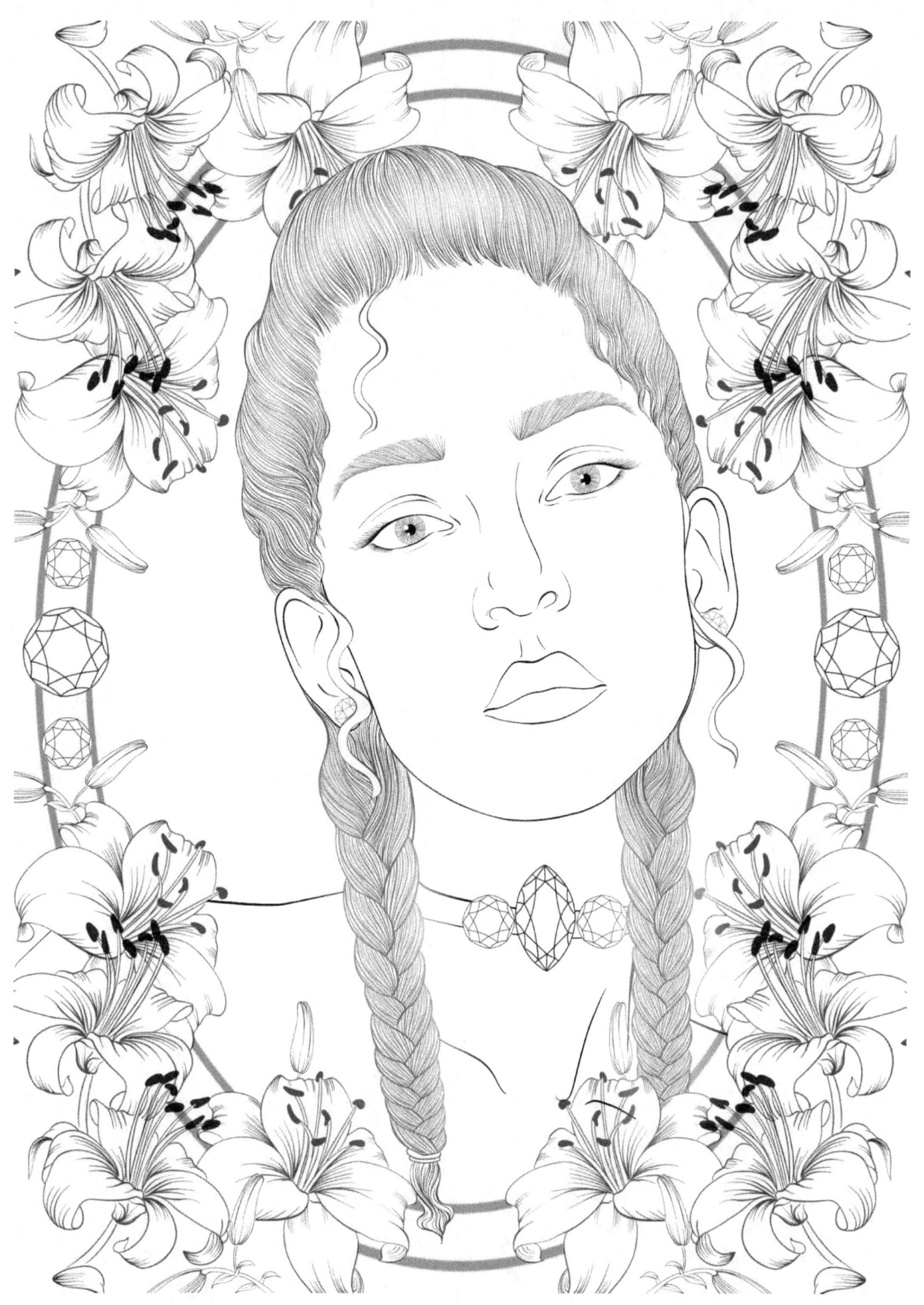

www.ingramcontent.com/pod-product-compliance
Lightning Source LLC
Chambersburg PA
CBHW062343220526
45469CB00008B/2815